Phil & Jenny,
Great to meet..
spend time with you!
Say hello to Atlanta for us.
And when you're ready to
move to Fort Lauderdale let us
help you.   Love & hugs!
K

I HATE
GETTING OLD!

*I need to find something to do with myself as I
get old, or I'm going to go crazy!*

Karl Gustafson

Book@theSpiritualElders.com

Dedication

The wisdom in this book largely comes from my numerous friends who died way too early from AIDS. They became sudden elders, before their time. This book is dedicated to them, with great sadness and many fond memories. I live my life out loud in tribute to them.

I wish I could recall all their names.

Louise Hay said "Honor the entirety of your journey. Don't wish any of it away. Use it for the betterment of the world."

I Hate Getting Old!
If I don't find something to do with myself, I'm going to go crazy

For information:

Karl Gustafson

184 Westminster Drive NE

Atlanta, Georgia 30309

Printed in the United States of America

Acknowledgments

One of the displays of abundance in my life that I am most proud of is my diverse group of loving friends. Through you I found my voice. Thank you! See you at the next full moon, you Lunatics!

My mate, so called because we both love all things ocean and we are mated for life, and I recently celebrated our 30th anniversary. I am proud of this because I know how much we have each put into making our relationship work for so long. I feel very fortunate to have Drew Cockrell in my life. Without his support and love this book wouldn't exist.

My parents worked hard to give me a special childhood much grander than either had themselves experienced. Their belief in the value of education gave me every advantage. They taught me what it is to be a good person. Thank you! I love you both!

My sister, Ann Sorice, and I have learned to be friends due in large part to her involving me in our mother's care in old age. I am so happy for and proud of my only sibling! Her husband, Sid, and three boys, Nick, Max and Lang, are incredible humans, whose love means the world to me. And my sister's father-in-law, John, is a wonderful example of an elder, and one I get to bounce ideas off of. I look forward to seeing each of us pursue our lives as the years pass, letting us continue to grow in wisdom and love.

My departed mentor, Tom Troendle, influenced me greatly, in both high and low pursuits. He was a source of thought-provoking wit and life-changing books, always quick to point out world assumptions that made no sense. I miss you, Tom! I look forward to running into you again, dear soul.

My high school art teacher Pat Foley kept me sane during awkward years, especially with his example of a life lived on his own terms. Thanks for being a rebel, a great example for me!

My summers in Colorado at Travis Anderson's camps exposed me to nature's beauty and massive scale, a love that has often served me well, calmed me down, and informed my questions. What a beautiful soul, taken away too soon.

Richard Rhodes and SAGE Atlanta led to many conversations about what it's like to be lifetime leaders always pushing the boundaries of society, just by living your own life. Keep it up!

Gert McMullin, the Goddess of the AIDS Quilt, is a dear friend who has seen more death than anyone I know. She readily shares the wisdom she has gained through our reminiscences of dance floors past. Our dogs are frequent playmates, and Gert spoils them rotten. Dance on!

Samuel Bowling, a new friend in my life, has held up his side of our metaphysical musings well, allowing my knowledge of the universe to grow and deepen. Best of wishes in the next chapter of your life. I'll miss you greatly, yet I look forward to many more adventures.

David Ault, senior minister at the Spiritual Living Center of Atlanta, my spiritual home, has educated me with his shared life stories to know that heart-felt knowledge is more valuable than logic. Love you David!

Jeffon Seely, a gifted speaker wise beyond his years, in writing his own book challenged me to write my own. I have learned so much from him already. I can hardly wait to see where Jeffon takes himself to, inspiring many lives on the way. Respect.

Diane Edwards provided a safe venue for me to start talking about the wisdom I'd gathered throughout my lifetime, planting the seed that has grown into this book, and beyond. Thank you!

Penelope LaPorte, a published medium, is a new friend whose life-story has informed and broadened my knowledge of the aging experience, especially from a spiritual outlook. She was the first one to read any of my manuscript and offered on-target advice. I look forward to us getting to know each other better.

The Spiritual Living Center of Atlanta has been my spiritual home since the first day I attended. The love there is palpable. I have grown so there, in my love for myself and in my comfort walking in the world. The staff, fellow congregants, and fellow Practitioners mean the world to me.

Karen Ratts is a fellow Practitioner at the Spiritual Living Center of Atlanta. In a phone call she helped me see that more of the universe would be available to me if I ventured further out into the universe. Life altering guidance that is already yielding results in my life. Namaste'!

One of the joys in my life has been our dogs. They have each had their own personalities and wisdom. I have talked more to them than to most of the humans in my life. Each a rescue, they have rescued me... Buster, Flipper and Boomerang

Thank you! Love and hugs!

Table of Contents

To download a copy of the Workbook that goes with this book please follow the link below:

https://tinyurl.com/I-Hate-Getting-Old-WORKBOOK

Thanks!

Getting Old Sucks!

Getting old sucks! Who in their right mind would want to get old?

Have you heard how old people are talked about, right in front of them, like they're not there? Have you seen how old people are depicted? They're a group that it's still acceptable to put down. What happened to the notion that old people should be venerated?

Margie has a big birthday approaching, and it's driving her crazy. She and her husband have prepared themselves financially for retirement, but she's not prepared emotionally. Her life has been full, balancing raising a family and her career, and her husband's career, too. Margie hasn't had the time to do much of the spiritual seeking that she relishes.

As Margie contemplates becoming an empty-nester and a retiree, both in the near future, she has a hard time envisioning herself as old. Her mother wasn't there to provide some sort of role model. But she certainly has many images of getting old from the media. She doesn't want to become a bag lady, or even a cat lady.

Normally Margie takes good care of herself, eating and sleeping soundly. Lately she's not been sleeping as well, often kept up at night by the dread of getting old. It seems like a time of loss and frailty. She dares not think about the alternative to getting old, the possibility of her death. She's really not prepared for that. She has a will, however it was written a long time ago, when they had their third son.

Margie's life has been full of meaning. Raising her boys has meant the world to her. Now they are so big, towering over their father, and two of them working. The time has gone so fast. She wonders if she's ready for a big change of pace, and of everything else? What can she do to prepare herself, so that the years ahead of her, which could be many, are full, too?

Climbing the career ladder gave Margie a path to follow, some long-term purpose. She still wants to feel that something is pulling her forward, and right now she doesn't see anything there. She wants to feel like she is still of use, to her family and to her community. She wants to continue to be valued for her contributions to society.

Today Margie feels lost, without a path forward. The thought of getting old is driving her crazy. She fears the changes that are ahead of her, to her body and mind. She doesn't see a place for herself in the community, and that is upsetting her, having worked so hard with her boys and her career. She is used to being well–regarded. She's seeking a way forward that also allows her to explore more of herself and her spirituality, subjects she's not had enough time, up until now, to really study.

Margie is angry at the world, feeling like the rules are suddenly changing. She's been doing everything she can to stay young–looking, including Botox. She resents having to go to such extremes to maintain her looks, but her co-workers get younger and younger. Sometimes Margie has a drink too many, and this is a new behavior. It helps to numb her fears, momentarily, but they are back in the morning, as are the creases in her forehead. It also helps quiet her mind, so she can get to sleep, something in short supply these days. Margie and her husband have been told they will be solid money-wise in retirement, but Margie still worries about running out. Have they really saved enough? Has anybody saved enough? She really doesn't want to have to move into an old folks' home.

A couple of Margie's close friends have died recently, both of cancer. It was awful to witness, the pain and worry. And the poor families left to mourn. Margie doesn't like to admit it, but she's afraid of dying. She's certain it's got to be an awful experience, for everyone involved, and painful, too. Nor is she thrilled at the prospect of getting sick as she gets old.

What will Margie do if her husband dies first, as men are likely to do? She's not been alone like that in a long time. Will she be able to take care of herself? She worries about keeping up their house.

Her worries have grown to the point of sapping Margie's energy, sometimes finding herself uncharacteristically depressed. There isn't any motivation available, for anything.

What I see for Margie is that she is on the path of spiritual aging, she just isn't aware of it. Her anger at her current situation is natural and healthy. She might stumble further along, but it is unlikely. She has a conscious choice to make, to continue to grow, or not. The seeker part of her is soon to be fully engaged, doing both inner and outer explorations. But that's only if she's made aware of the future that's possible and she chooses to move in that direction. This is new territory and the path isn't all sweetness and light. A guide would help.

This book is that guide. Reading it, and contemplating what it says to you, as you are today, an elder in training, will lead you on the path of spiritual eldering. As Robert Browning said: "Grow old along with me. The best is yet to be."

Not only do I see the continued evolution of someone into an elder as a good thing for that person, I see it as a good thing for humanity. Demographic forces are raising the numbers of potential elders, as are longer lifetimes. Currently about 10,000 people a day are turning 70, and this will continue for the next 20 years. As this swelling population is coming forward, the times are calling them forward. Elderhood has been forgotten long enough. Only very recently have we seen the ability to feed the world. In Western cultures we are seeing obesity become the norm. We don't yet know what to do with all our abundance. We don't know what to do with the nuclear bombs we've invented which can now wipe out humanity many times over. We don't know how to best manage a world of 7^+ billion souls that is now more connected than ever.

Today's seniors, tomorrow's elders, are the most traveled, most educated and the richest generation of humans in all of history. Given the chance, they have the ability to solve some of today's pressing problems, using their uniquely elder skills. Their corporate training and life lessons will serve them well, too.

When I think of what's to come I think of an old Jonny Carson show. He was having a hard time getting his first guest to talk much. She had just turned a hundred years old and had known many famous people during her life. Jonny finally said to her "Well, who's the most famous person you've known?" She quickly responded "Tommy, Tommy Edison. But that was before he invented electricity!" To think that this woman was now on television, the highest expression thus far of Edison's electricity and she knew life before electricity. That blows my mind, thinking of all she's seen, and contemplating how much we'll see in our lifetimes, given all that we have seen already...

(If you would like to have the Workbook that goes with this book, please follow this link:
https://tinyurl.com/I-Hate-Getting-Old-WORKBOOK)

Who am I?

I have always been drawn to the oldest person in the room, for as long as I can remember. I think it was more because they were easy people to talk to. They were patient with me and didn't want to run off to find something more exciting. They would listen to my half-formed stories. In turn, I got to hear amazing tales of the lives they'd led, the wisdom they wished to impart.

When I was learning to drive an English friend of my father gave me this advice: "You can go as fast as you want, as long as you have a quiet muffler." I was already a quiet child, but this put words to one of my philosophies of life. Plus, it was true of driving. Part of being a good listener, to get the best stories from deep down, is to provide the teller with assurance that their story won't be repeated. I continue to be astounded by what people will tell me if I ask, because I'm known for being able to keep a secret. To this day one of my delights is to have a person tell me the story of their life, what made them the person they are today. I feel very privileged to have heard many. And everyone has a story worth listening to, or three.

My family moved around a lot when I was young. My father was in heavy construction and we were following jobs around the world. I was born in suburban New Jersey. When I was six-months-old we moved to Puerto Rico, where I liked to play in the rain. At age one, we moved to London, where I liked to chase pigeons. At two we moved to Monrovia, Liberia, in West

Africa, and our backyard backed up to jungle. We moved back to Cranford, New Jersey, where I had to unlearn some foreign customs, when I was four-and-a-half. All the moving left me good at adapting to new circumstances and great at observing what was going on around me.

In Africa, I contracted a disease in my legs that required me to be in a cast from my waist to my toes, immobilizing my hips. I had to ask for help to do most everything, including going to the bathroom. I came to resent having to ask for help, not being able to take care of myself and needing to ask for assistance. What I found was that by listening to what people said to me and around me I could learn a lot about what was going on with them. This made it easier for me to open a conversation with them, using my gathered information. I could also slide in my request for help into a paragraph, instead of it having to be the headline.

I have been told more than once that I listen "too well." I sometimes hear things that people did not know they were telling me. Putting together seemingly unrelated information, and subtly testing my hypothesis with simple questions, I am able to deduce unspoken wisdom. It took getting in trouble many times before I learned that I don't need to share everything I have learned in this manner. I had thought by letting someone know that I had heard them, they would appreciate being really listened to. More often they were upset, wanting to know how I knew what I knew. Today I have learned to trust my intuitions and to let them remain unsaid, most of the time. Dolly Parton has a song about an old witch, entitled *These Old Bones*, that helped guide the refinement of my use of the insights I gain in this manner.

As an example, for much of the 1990s I was renovating a public market in Downtown Atlanta. The building was owned by the city but operated by a separate non-profit, which I ran for 7 years. We were reliant on Federal grants administered by the city for our capital funding. At a City Council meeting I met a man who had been with the city his whole career, knowing the grant programs like no one else, about to retire, and professing to have a life-long love of the Curb Market. I soon called him to set up a lunch meeting to pick his brain about getting more grants.

At lunch we talked a lot about the Market, with him sharing many stories of shopping there throughout his lifetime. I was loving the conversation. Every once in a while, he would mention something personal. I began to notice a pattern, that all the places he mentioned were gay meccas, like New Orleans, San Francisco and Provincetown. I asked a few questions probing a little deeper occasionally to test my hypothesis. Before long I concluded that he was gay. I had previously learned, from bad experiences, that people didn't like to be called out by a total stranger. I think they feel it's like Big Brother is watching them. So, I did nothing with that information, except for listen with a more finely tuned ear to all that he had to say.

At the end of lunch, he invited me to dinner. I responded by asking if I could bring my mate. He got flustered and left without answering. I went back to my desk and worried that I had blown any chances of the Market getting any more grant money. Thirty minutes later the phone rang. He called to set a time to meet for dinner. Yay! Relief!

Another aspect of my powers of observation may come from being a gay man in a "straight" world. Well before having a name for it, I felt different. Worrying that my parents would reject me if they found out, and certain that my difference was a "bad" thing, further sharpened my observation skills. I was always on the lookout for someone figuring me out. There's a book, entitled *The Best Boy in the World.*, written under a pseudonym by a friend of mine, which describes a gay child's strategy of being good to act as a counterweight to their innate badness. That was my strategy, too.

As I have come to accept my being gay, I have also realized gifts in it. As a white male I have rarely had a problem being let into "the room." That did not mean I felt like I belonged there, though. I have often felt like an included observer, able to see the big picture, and the details, "in the world, but not of it."

About the time I started to accept myself as gay the CDC published the first-ever press release about what has come to be known as AIDS. The specter of an early death has been with me my entire adult life. When the first test for the AIDS came out in 1985, I wanted to know my fate. The deaths I was aware of at that point had been painful and abrupt. They usually included families very upset to find out in the same breath that their son was dying and gay, many abandoning their sons. I determined I did not want to go through the same thing, preferring to commit suicide if I tested positive. I bought a fast motorcycle with the idea of crashing it into a wall if necessary. When I tested negative, thank God, I didn't know what to do with the motorcycle.

In the early 1990s, my work days would start with reading the obituaries in the newspaper. I kept a piece of paper in my desk drawer listing my friends around the country who had died of AIDS, at least the ones I knew of. When the list covered both sides of the paper, three columns on each side, I angrily wadded it up and threw it in the trash. Unfortunately, that was not the end of the deaths. Today I wish I had that piece of paper, because I know there are names I have forgotten.

Contemplating my own death and witnessing the death of over 200 friends before age 40 has given me a great appreciation for the gift of life. I know that we are each going to die, that we must live each day as if it may be our last one; we never know when it might be our time, AIDS or not. I firmly believe that the best thing that I can do to remember all these lives cut short is to live my life to the fullest, not in mourning, out loud. I wonder if others who have not seen so much death necessarily value life as I do. I like what Auntie Mame said: "Live, live, live! Life is a banquet and most poor suckers are starving to death!" I gained a lot of wisdom, at an awful cost, from watching friends quickly change from vibrant adults to people at the end of their lives. They had lots in mind for the future, and suddenly found out it wasn't going to happen.

That knowledge has prompted me to live each day more presently and more fully.

Thich Nhat Hanh puts it this way: "We are very good preparing to live, but not very good at living. We know how to sacrifice ten years for a diploma, and we are willing to work very hard to get a job, a car, a house, and so on. But we have difficulty remembering that we are alive in the present moment, the only moment there is for us to be alive."

Today I have many friends who are long-term survivors of AIDS. Most are thriving, living full lives, but some are still dying. A very close friend and mentor ended his own life three years ago. He preferred to not end up an invalid. After a minor stroke, related to years of harsh medicine, he was afraid he would become unable to take care of himself.

About 15 years ago my father started showing signs of dementia. His golf buddies noticed it first. He was no longer able to keep their daily scorecard. Initially it was thought that his trouble was due to a series of small strokes. As his dementia progressed my parents moved into senior housing, with the idea that if he needed more help than my mother could provide it would be available. The first time I visited their community I had a visceral reaction, of not liking the place, even though it really was a nice facility. Since then I have devoted much of my life towards making sure seniors are able to live their lives to the fullest. Initially I was called to work on reinventing senior housing, to have it refined for my generation, the Baby Boomers. My research led me to find that there were more aspects to aging than just housing that effected seniors' quality of life.

Eventually my father's dementia was diagnosed as Alzheimer's. My mother bore the brunt of it as his caregiver. I was half-way across the country and only saw him occasionally. Initially my visits didn't go very well. Some of the statements his addled mind made were rough on me. To some extent my mother kept me away from him, much to my chagrin, even though I realized that she was doing it to protect me from his harsh words.

After a while he became quieter, only speaking sometimes when spoken to. I was able to make peace with my father during this time. We had never been close before. With his work travel he was physically absent a lot of the time. His own father had not been emotionally present for him, and he repeated that past with me, when he was around. In his diminished state I could sit with him and just be. If he would let me, I'd hold his hand some of the time I sat with him.

I was also able to come to a level of peace with the idea that I, too, may come down with Alzheimer's. A lot of my spiritual work is becoming more conscious of my own inner workings and the world's. We don't really know what Alzheimer's is like from the inside, we can only guess. I now see it as another stage of consciousness to be explored, if it comes to that. I don't mean to minimize the impact the terrible disease has on the loved ones left as caregivers. I can only surmise how hard it was on my mother, health-wise and emotionally. But I don't fear it as much as I once did.

By the time my father died I knew that he loved me and that he knew I loved him. His life, devoted to providing for me and my family, and his death have fueled my inquiry as to what can make the last years of life the best years of life.

Several years ago, I joined the Atlanta chapter of a national group called SAGE, Services and Advocacy for GLBTQ Elders. We concluded that we were having difficulty finding new members because people didn't see themselves "old enough" to be elders. Doing my own research, I found out about rites of passage that marked becoming a tribal elder or crone. This piqued my interest greatly. Finding little written about actual ceremonies, I was challenged to come up with my own rites of passage into elderhood. I want people so excited about becoming an elder, getting older consciously, that they want to throw themselves a party.

What I have seen is that there is a difference in being old and being an elder. One is counting birthdays until you die. The other is thriving, like never before, freer than ever to explore what brings you joy and where you see beauty. One is a life void of purpose and meaning, while the other is a new and valued role in your community.

Possibilities

Elizabeth Kubler Ross has written about the stages of grief: denial, anger, bargaining, depression and acceptance. The grief that they apply to isn't only that of someone else dying, but also to times when parts of us die along the way, such as when we must let go of a part of our self-image. As part of the human condition, for most of people's lives they walk around in denial of their own aging. This is part of the ego's self-preservation role.

Denial of aging can take many forms. Some just never contemplate the idea of themselves ever getting old. Others do everything they can to not appear to age, including what they wear and do, relentless exercising, pursuing younger partners and even plastic surgery. Advertising along the lines of "60 is the new 40," or the extreme I've seen: "100 is the new 65," are appealing to this tendency towards denial of your aging.

The trouble with remaining in denial of your aging is that you are not able to really get in touch with whatever good is available. It takes energy to deny reality time and again. That's energy that could be used elsewhere, like for living a contented life, even as you age.

Like with other changes in your life's direction, the first step is awareness that you are in denial. Being in denial then isn't a bad thing. What's not productive is being unaware of it. What's good about life is that it doesn't ever stop sending signs. Once a sign catches your consciousness, following ones will have an easier time breaking through. Often the death of a parent, or some other harsh jolt, brings your own denial into awareness. I know that happened to me, with the death of my father. Suddenly, my own aging came into focus, I couldn't deny it anymore.

Denial is the first in Kubler-Ross' stages of acceptance. The next step is anger. With aging, that is some form of being angry about the prospect of getting old. Gruff seniors are common enough to be a stereotype, or even a movie. You've seen seniors expressing their frustration about not being seen, for example, at the store where clerks seem to ignore them. They speak loudly and gruffly, like they are very angry. I've been ignored like that, and it did not sit well with me. I've read that that type of anger is learned. Seniors adopt it as a way of being heard and seen; it's not that they are angry people. The anger I mean is deeper than that, angry at the world. Our expectations of how life will play out have been shaken. Life isn't treating us anymore the way we have grown used to it. We haven't changed but the way the world treats us has. And that makes us angry.

At this stage it's good to find constructive ways of expressing/releasing this anger. Finding a time and place where I can scream at the top of my lungs helps me immensely. That anger is being held in your body, where it will stay until it is released. A variation on screaming is conscious breathing. I once ran into a friend of mine. He was visibly shaken. He had just left an abusive relationship and was feeling quite lost and alone. We fell into breathing together, timing our breaths to each other's quickly. After a few minutes of this he let out a huge sigh. Without a word we acknowledged what we had both felt, a big relief from where he had been. Another "safe" expression of anger is hitting a pillow, again until the anger has been released. Without such a release the anger will remain inside.

The next step is bargaining. What can I keep from before, and what am I willing to cede to the aging process. Just because you can no longer play tennis as a top seeded single doesn't mean you have to give up tennis; you could join the doubles league instead. Just because you can no longer walk as well as you used to, or even walk at all, doesn't mean you have to give up living. This is a vital stage as you realize what is still important to you, and what isn't so much. This may be your first such self-assessment in a while, maybe the first ever. You may find that some things which you stopped doing to become a busy and productive adult are now important to you again. You may even find some skills that you didn't realize you had. In this process you are formulating a new you. It's more an adaptation, though, than a re-invention.

Mahatma Gandhi put it this way: "As human beings our greatness lies not so much in our ability to remake the world...but in our ability to remake ourselves." This may not be the first time you've remade yourself, but it is likely to be the most conscious one. When I look back on my own life, every time I moved to a new city I had a chance to remake myself, picking what I wanted to emphasize and what I wished to jettison.

At the end of 8th Grade I knew I was moving to Houston that summer, starting over in a new place. On my last day of school, when I was saying my good-byes one 7th grader pulled me aside to say that he suspected that I was gay. I was mortified. In hindsight, perhaps he noticed me because he was gay, too... When I moved to Houston I wanted to be straight, not one bit gay, and I vowed to not do anything gay there. For the most part I did not, at least not until after moving back to Houston after Yale.

The last step you reach in the grieving process before acceptance is depression. Whoopee, depression! It won't make it any easier knowing you are almost there, but you are. The depression is mourning your old self, your old life, even after the bargains you've made with yourself. It's a valid and necessary stage to go through, as unappealing as such sadness sounds. It's not a step to skip, even if you want to. Stuffed down things tend to pop back up, usually in a more strident way. Nor am I saying to wallow in it. Go through the valley, just don't buy a condominium there.

One caveat to be said with Kubler-Ross' stages of grief and acceptance is that they rarely go perfectly in order, and they may overlap. If you find yourself depressed before you've really bargained with your aging that's alright, you're not an odd duck, it's normal. You may even skip a stage, lucky you. Or one may hit you particularly hard. It is important, though, to let the process play itself out, to not try to hurry it along.

The grieving here, mourning the loss of a self-image you've held, is different than that associated with the loss of a loved one. For example, this grief will be more solitary. No one else will be mourning the same loss. When someone dies, usually you are one of their family members, or one of their friends; you are part of a group effected by the same loss. This loss is also not a total loss, as it is when someone leaves this plane of existence. "You" are still around, it's just that you've changed, evolved. Socrates offers this advice: "The secret to change is to focus all of your energy, not on fighting the old, but on building the new."

Acceptance is the last step. You have realized you were in denial about your aging; gotten angry about it; bargained with yourself about what is still important and what is not; and, gotten depressed over the changes that are happening. Now you are ready to incorporate this new aspect of yourself into your whole being. It isn't all of you, but it is a valid and important part.

This may feel akin to puberty. For most of us, that time, and the changes it brought, was a process that sometimes went fast and sometimes went slow. Sometimes it was very disconcerting and uncomfortable. While there are physical changes that take place with aging, the process of self-acceptance this time is more of a mind evolution, than a body one. But it can be just as ungainly at times as you were in puberty. And the body has its own set of changes. Feeling those changes will not be optional.

Is the process done now? I'm afraid not. Bill Thomas, a world-renowned innovator with regards to aging, says that there are three attitudes towards aging: denial, acceptance and enthusiasm. The process of grief will move you from denial, the state most people are in, to acceptance. But what will move you from acceptance to enthusiasm? Is it even possible to become enthusiastic about aging?

As a modern society we are familiar with the life-stages of youth and adult. What we have forgotten is the third stage of life, that of the elder. Some people place the loss of the elder stage with the industrial revolution, when urban life started to become the norm. Others put it with the coming of agriculture, which allowed cities to begin to flourish. With both, and the wealth that they generated, family structures changed. It used to be that everyone lived in the family compound, youths, adults and elders. There wasn't the possibility of moving out when you wanted to; there weren't the resources nor the houses. Either way, the elder stage has been part of human existence most of our time on earth. It is only recently that it has been forgotten.

In sociology they talk about the "grandmother effect." Comparing a tribe with grandmothers present versus one without them, the one with them will progress at a faster rate than one without. What they provide: nurturing, care and wisdom, benefit their tribe noticeably, especially their granddaughters. This used to happen because all the generations lived together, under one roof. I'm sure you noticed that it's not named after grandfathers, even in our patriarchal society. There are two reasons for that. First, most men did not survive adulthood; it was only women who did for the most part. Second, women's elderhood is tied to menopause, when women go from being able to bear children to not being able to do so. For most mammals, females remain fertile, capable of childbearing, until they die. In humans that is not the case. The elder role is an evolutionary one, built into women's bodies. Men get to go along, too, in their own way, to become elders in their own rights, as do those of us who don't have children.

What is an elder? It is not defined solely by age. "Elders are not born, they are not appointed, they emerge as the sum total of the experience of life, they are a state of being," per S. M. Stiegelbauer. To Inuit Native Americans an elder is someone who has put down the busy-ness of being an adult. They possess a broad vision, built on experience. They are loving and caring and give whatever help is needed. They lead highly spiritual lives and "walk the talk." They take a public role as the keepers of history and wisdom. In Hindu culture Yogis have the primary role of reconnecting people to the natural world, to its rhythms and wisdom, from which people living their busy lives have become disconnected. Among Aboriginal communities, elders share a deep spirituality, which they prefer to teach by example, living highly principled lives. In Canada's First Nation "the individual has had enough life experience to have something to offer those behind them. In a sense Elders are 'experts on life.'"

Elderhood is the fullest expression of human evolution. For those who choose to become elders it is often the best time of their lives. By embracing becoming an elder you can move from acceptance to enthusiasm about your aging.

Many people worry about having a life of meaning and purpose past adulthood. We are familiar with the role of an adult, creating a family and working to provide for it. Elders have a role in community also, and it is a public one, not a go-off-to-the-woods one. They are the ones who possess a long-view, able to see generations back; they are the keepers of the history; they are the caretakers of fellow elders and the youth, and sometimes of the adults, too; they are the ones who by their own lives demonstrate spirituality in action.

Elderhood is a more about being than the doing of adulthood. Physical changes can contribute to this change in focus. It is an ideal time to deepen your spirituality, whatever that means to you. To me this is the real gold in elderhood, to explore the Universe and my own place in it.

Reading this book and taking the time to think about becoming an elder, will lead you down a path of self-discovery. Do you want to become "an expert at life?"

Your Jubilee!

You have likely celebrated several rites of passage, although you may not have recognized them as such. A rite of passage is defined as "an important act or event that serves to mark a passage from one stage of life to another." Graduating high school, graduating college, getting married, and having a child are a few rites of passage that you may have already experienced in your life, among others.

Rites of passage, like the concept of elderhood, have fallen out of fashion with modern humans. Some blame the industrial revolution for this, yet for others it goes back to the dawn of civilization, stepping away from our tribal roots. It used to be common for many more rites of passage to be celebrated, and for those to be celebrated differently than they are now. Rites of puberty used to involve months of preparation, and the final rite was attended by everyone in the village, baby to elder. They were designed to not only mark the celebrant's life change but also to entertain the celebrators. Such rites were integral to the life of the village. The stories that were told at these rites instructed the members about their responsibilities to each other, taught their shared history, and shaped the ethos of the group. Such rites also allowed for a release of energy from the group, necessary for the ongoing well-being of the community.

Rites of passage usually have three successive parts. The first part is separation, losing one's current identity. Then there is a transition, often involving testing and education, passing on customs, skills and tribal knowledge, shaping the new identities. The last part, incorporation, involves the rest of your family and community. A ceremony or meal brings the celebrants back into the community with their new roles, sometimes including new jewelry, clothing or names as emblems of their new status.

One rite of passage that we have lost is the one marking the transition of an adult into the new role of tribal elder. The closest we still have to that is a retirement party, which while it marks the end of a role it does nothing to prepare one to become an elder. As has been noted previously, one does not become an elder just by reaching a certain age, it's more than that. It's recognition by one's peers of having already stepped into the different role of an elder, having a broad perspective from decades of experience, and using that perspective to the benefit of one's tribe.

My own research has turned up little about eldering ceremonies, so I have created some of my own, as have others. Ron Pevney, author of *Conscious Living – Conscious Aging*, conducts week-long retreats that are a form of eldering ceremonies. I look forward to participating in one with him soon!

A jubilee is defined by Oxford as "a special anniversary of an event..." One rite of passage that I have come up with is a Jubilee Party, to celebrate one's entry into elderhood. It's a party you throw for yourself. It can be at your home, but it is recommended that you hold it at a friend's home or at a restaurant or club that has a private room. The reason for not doing it at your own home is then you will have less to be concerned with the night of the party. You will be the star and will want to spend your time enjoying yourself, not worried about the food or the lighting. If you are going to do it at your home, you'll want to have it catered, if possible.

Whether you are going to have the party at your home or somewhere else, you will need to appoint one of your guests as a lieutenant, someone to assist you the night of the event.

The first items on the preparations list are to identify the guest list, to set a date (about 8 weeks out) and to line up the location. These three elements each influence the other, so they should be done together. With the guest list it's important to only include people you want to have in your future. You don't have to invite the entire village or tribe.

Another early decision is whether to plan a sit-down dinner or passed hors d'oeuvres. A sit-down dinner with a round or square table is preferred, but only if you have a table that will fit all your guests. Otherwise you will want to set up the room with a circle of chairs, enough for all your guests, plus you and your lieutenant.

For the party you will need two outfits. The first one can be a favorite of yours now, or a new one. This is to be worn for the first half of the party. During the dessert course, you will change into the second outfit, this one new if at all possible. This one will be representative of the new elder, you, so if you are considering a change in wardrobe with your new role, this is where to start. Again, if at all possible, you will want to also have a new piece of (visible) jewelry to go with the second outfit. It's another symbol of a new you. The party will be a splurge, but you shouldn't break the bank in doing so.

The night of the party you will have your lieutenant greet your guests as they arrive. Once everyone has arrived have your lieutenant ask everyone to be seated, whether around a table for dinner or in a circle around the room. Be sure everyone has a drink and start serving the food.

At this point you will want to make your first entrance, in the first outfit, with as little fanfare as possible, taking the vacant seat left in the circle.

Once you are seated and settled in, your lieutenant will call the guests to attention to announce the next phase of the ceremony. Each person will have the opportunity to share a favorite story about you, starting with your lieutenant, likely the only person there prepared to do so. Then it will proceed counter-clockwise around the circle, with each person given a chance to talk.

It is important that you do not respond, other than with a "thank you" to what is said. They are telling stories about the old you. Your role is to listen with an open heart to what is said, taking it all in.

Once the stories have been completed, dessert is served, either at the table or around the circle. At this time, you will leave the room, again as quietly as possible.

Now it's time to change into the second outfit, and to put on your new jewelry, if that's part of the rite.

Reappearing, again quietly, in your new outfit, signals the next step in the rite of passage. In as many, or as few, words as you would like and feel comfortable, it's time for you to tell the gathered crowd what you see for the next stage of your life. It's time to talk about your vision for your life as an elder in this community.

After that is when you can mingle with your guests, now as an elder (in-training?).

The day after your party I'd like for you to send me an email to Book@theSpiritualElders.com. I'd like you to tell me about your party, and how it made you feel. What did you learn?

While you are planning your own Jubilee, you can finish the rest of the book, and do more of the work that will lead you to becoming an elder.

It's all good

"It's all good" has recently been a common pat response, which usually meant just the opposite. It was more like the song "It's not right but it's OK." Neville Goddard would term "It's all good" a conscious assumption. It is an assumption because you don't know if it is true or not, you are just assuming it is. We all operate our lives based on many assumptions, they're the human operating system. But most of them are unconscious, we aren't aware that we have made them. What is different about this one for me is that I have made this assumption consciously.

"It's all good" has been the motto of my spiritual practice for the last several years. No matter what comes up it's my first conscious response, at least most of the time. Seeing it as bad would lead me to searching for someone else to blame or to find the cause a weakness within myself. That's a lot of time and energy spent unproductively. It could be better spent formulating an appropriate response, or no response at all. I went through a long period of self-analysis, looking for answers as to why some things seemed true for me. A friend, a skilled therapist, said that even if we knew why you did something that wouldn't change it. The process wasn't a waste of time, I got to know myself better. Now when something comes up I've learned to not worry about figuring out the why.

In *The Tempest* William Shakespeare wrote that "There is nothing either good or bad, but thinking makes it so." Nothing is inherently good or bad, they are just labels we put on things, labels you choose. Most of the time the labeling is unconscious, based on your unconscious assumptions. You have unconscious assumptions about what other people think is good or bad, thinking that most others hold the same beliefs you do, even though that may not be the case.

A high-school friend of mine would often say "That's what you get for thinking!" in response to a statement that began "but I thought..." You can spend hours, days, months, years, even a lifetime, thinking about something that happened. And complaining about it too, how someone did you wrong, or of a tragic mistake you made. Doing so takes you away from living, from life itself.

"It's all good" is part of accepting what is, instead of thinking about it, fighting with it. But it's more than that because beyond just acceptance it is also putting a positive spin on things. It is labeling something, but with a consistent "good" label. Accepting what is doesn't mean trivializing everything. What if there is some knowledge to be gained from the experience? Not spending your time finding the root cause or someone to blame frees up time to examine the wisdom to be gained from the experience. You may find an assumption that is now conscious. By making it conscious you can examine it and see if you still agree with it. If you don't, you can consciously change the assumption.

For example, let's say that I assume my speedometer is correct. If the GPS on my phone indicates a faster speed than the one registered on the speedometer I have a choice to make. Which one will I assume is correct from here on? A police officer is not likely to take kindly to the excuse that my speedometer is wrong and that's why I was speeding. If I assume that the GPS is right, I can adjust my readings on the speedometer, so as to obey the speed limit, or at least only speed as much as I am comfortable speeding.

Marie Curie, the noted scientist, said it this way: "Nothing in life is to be feared, it is only to be understood." Again, nothing is inherently "bad," or feared, and there is knowledge to be found in the examination thereof. She went on to say, "Now is the time to understand more, so that we may fear less." That "now" can be taken two ways. One is that the time to tease out the lesson in something that just happened is right then, right after it has happened to you; now, currently, not later. The other now is right now, in it's time now to start accepting what is and making the conscious assumption that "It's all good" now, today, from this second of your life forward.

In Brene Brown's book *Rising Strong*, she examines the proposition that everyone is doing the best they can at that moment. Her husband's take on it is that his life is easier if he makes that conscious assumption. He is able to constructively examine his reaction instead of dwelling on the why and the pain. And don't we all want easier lives?

Buddhist teaching tells us that if you focus on the hurt, you will continue to suffer. If you label something as bad it will continue to be an irritant. But if you focus on the lesson, you will continue to grow. If you make the conscious assumption that it is good and examine it for its lesson, you will gain more wisdom.

A classmate of mine talked about training herself to say this whenever something that initially looked challenging came up: "I cannot wait to see what good comes of this!" She looks for the good in everything, even things that most people would label as "bad." As events play out the good may become clear, or it may not. Either way, she can go on without getting stuck.

"It's all good" is still the focus of my spiritual practice today. In part that means that I am not yet consistently having it as my first response. Sometimes I find it hard to maintain that outlook, especially when people whom I care about cannot stop talking about the bad in life, complaining. But a lot of the time there is no conscious response, I just let things go without examination, knowing that my soul has absorbed the lesson, the wisdom.

I got to spend a summer in London during college. My family moved there for a short period when my father was heading his company's European office. "Over there" they drive on the opposite side of the road. When I first got there I almost got hit by a car every time I tried to cross the street. I was looking the wrong way the one I was used to in the States. Then I went through a stage where I would deliberately look the opposite way I went to instinctively look first, correcting myself. This helped for a while, and then it did not. Unconsciously I had already made the shift to looking the first time to the correct side. The correction of my first impulse was having me look the wrong way again. Then I went to the final stage of trusting my instincts to have me look the correct way.

I was already "enlightened" before I knew I was. So perhaps, I can find something else to focus my spiritual quest on, having seemingly mastered "It's all good." On the other hand, I could use more practice holding my thought despite of what others are saying or doing...

Choice

In the movie *The Matrix* Keanu Reeves' character is given life-changing information about how the world operates. Then he is given a choice of a red pill or a blue pill. One will return him to his previous existence, free of this new knowledge; the other pill will change him and the course of his life forever. When we come upon new information we have the same choice; we can go on acting like we don't know it, or we can incorporate it into a more complete understanding of how the world really is and our place in it.

I can recall times in my life when such a change happened, and I was consciously aware of reorganizing my mind around the new information. As things came up it seemed like I rewrote the mental index cards with the new information. It's like moving to a new home in the same part of town. More than once you'll drive "home" only to find that you've gone to the old house, which was "home" instead of to the new one which really is "home." How many times will you write down the wrong address?

If you have come to realize that you are in denial about aging, it is important to remember that you have a choice in how you take from here. You can choose to remain in denial, going along with the general flow. Making that decision doesn't mean that more reminders aren't going to keep coming. Have you ever thought to count all the grains of sand on a beach, or all the leaves on a tree? Nature also demonstrates this abundance in the number of reminders it sends to say, "you are aging, whether or not you acknowledge it." Or you can take it on, choosing to once again grow, to continue to evolve. You can choose a life of counting birthdays until you die, or you can choose to blossom into the fullest expression of the unique person that you are. Never before has there been someone with your gifts, your experiences, your genetic history, and your place in time. And there's more growth to be had.

As a young man in the late 1960s I was very fortunate to go to summer camp in Western Colorado, before Colorado had been discovered by so many travelers. The camp was located on the Colorado River and rafting was a daily option. Eventually I learned to kayak, too. A raft isn't very maneuverable, but it's very stable and you can bounce off rocks and such. A kayak, however, is very easy to turn, but it's tippy, too. If you're good at it, you can learn to roll the kayak back up if you do capsize. This makes it a sports car relative to the school buses rafts are to maneuver.

Rafts and kayaks are very different to paddle. One of the first things to learn is that if you're in a kayak you must lean downstream when entering the river. Otherwise the current will grab the upstream bottom of the boat and tip you over. Dunked into cold river water is not a great way to start the day. It takes some time to be able to paddle a kayak in a straight line, balancing the power of each stroke. My instructor, Mike Frazier, warned us that "in order to maneuver you must paddle faster than the current." If you just go with the flow, it will take you into rocks and trees and rapids. What you want to do instead is to paddle, propelling yourself faster than the current and down the best course of rapids, for the ride of your life. Or you could just float along with the current, like another piece of flotsam or jetsam.

Living your life is like that, too. The ability to "go with the flow" is highly rated. But the way to be able to maneuver through life's rapids is to "paddle faster than the current." That way you have a choice in where you go, what you experience. That doesn't mean you cannot hang out in the current and just drift along, some of the time, or maybe most of the time. But when something comes up, or is coming up, put your paddle back in the water and row, make a choice as to where you want to go, where you want to end up. I don't mean to imply that physical effort is needed. What is required is consciousness, being aware, being awake, *not* being in denial. That is how you paddle faster than the current of life.

If you don't think that this applies to you because you never have gone kayaking and never will, try this while driving. If you need to make a lane change when you're driving on the freeway, instead of slowing down to wait for a slot to open, try speeding up a little. I find it makes it easier, "paddling" faster than the current.

When I get stuck in a rut and forget that I have choices, it can feel like the entire world in conspiring against me, keeping me glued there. Sometimes that rut can last for days, weeks, months, even years. It can feel like it's my fate, cast in stone. A quote from Ralph Waldo

Emerson helps me when I've found myself there in a rut again – "the only person you are destined to become is the person you decide to be." In other words, you always have a choice, you can always decide, no matter what age or what circumstances you're in, that you are ready to have a different experience than the one you are having now, with aging or with anything else.

Another quote, this one from Joseph Campbell, inspires me with regards to my having choices: "the big question is whether you are going to say a hearty yes to your adventure." You have a choice, the red pill or the blue pill? Are you going to embrace your aging and do so consciously, or not? Can you see your aging as an adventure to be lived fully?

You are always at choice. You always can change your mind, too, to make a different choice. I was taught that making mistakes was a bad thing. It took me some time to realize that changing my mind was not a mistake, it was evolution. I still sometimes struggle with feelings that I have to stick with my original choice. What I am doing in changing my mind is updating my choice to make sense with the information I have currently.

People get in trouble when they get stuck and forget they have a choice. Suicide is the extreme expression of this, being able to see a world only in black and white, no gray and no escape. But what I have witnessed is how much a person's outlook on life can change in an instant when they are reminded that they do, in fact, have a choice.

When I was buying my first sports utility vehicle, a Jeep Cherokee Laredo, the first dealership only had 2-wheel=drive ones. I really wanted 4-wheel-drive. The salesman told me that "All four-wheel-drive means is that you're further from help when you need it." That's how I am with thinking about something sometimes. I'll find myself pretty far out there in my mental arguments with the Universe, before I realize I need help getting back to center.

Remembering that you always have a choice is strong, and wise.

Letting Go

It is said that holding a grudge against someone is like drinking poison and hoping your antagonist dies from the poison you ingested. Doing so hurts you much more than it hurts them, if it hurts them at all. The energy that a grudge takes eats away at you, not at them. The way to free yourself up from such poison is to let the grudge go.

Easier said than done, you say? Easy and hard are labels as much as good and bad are. Letting something go can be easy, too. All you have to do is let go of it.

The 900-year-old Jedi knight Yoda said this: "Train yourself to let go of everything you fear to lose." So, what are you afraid you are going to lose? Your youth? Your children? Your mate? Your home? Your health? There's a list of things to start letting go of.

Letting go of something does not mean totally erasing it from your life. What it means is letting go of attachment to it. If you derive your self-definition from some aspect of it still, you are attached to it, and it to you. If an incident still gives you a charge when you retell it, you're attached to it.

Snorkeling off Commercial Beach in Ft. Lauderdale, one of the creatures that you are likely to miss unless you know where to look for it is the decorator crab. The way to find one often is to find a dollar bill on the seafloor. Money deteriorates very slowly, by design, thus once it falls in the water it's there for a while.

Decorator crabs are so-called because the disguise themselves by collecting debris off the bottom and putting it onto their sticky backs. Usually it's bits of seashells and other items you'd normally find there, making them almost invisible. It's the odd things, like dollar bills, that give them away. We are like decorator crabs with our experiences in life, sticking them to ourselves. If the crab never let go of any of the debris on its back it would eventually die under the weight. So will you, if you don't learn to let go of things. We will not live a full life weighted down by all that baggage.

Is letting go scary? It can be. Think of this poem by Cynthia Occelli; "*For a seed to achieve its greatest expression, it must come completely undone. The shell cracks, the insides come out and everything changes. To someone who doesn't understand growth, it would look like complete destruction."*

What are some other things you can work on letting go of? From Sue Fitzmaurice: "Stop being offended. Let go of the need to win. Let go of the need to be right. Let go of the need to be superior. Let go of the need to have more. Let go of identifying yourself by your achievements. Let go of your reputation."

Along those same lines is letting go of judging others and yourself. It's much easier to judge someone than it is to really think about where they are and to empathize with them. We are worse with ourselves than we are when judging others. Let this all go. It's all good anyway! Right?

For many, getting old allows them to let go of some of society's rules. For women especially, it can be a time of incredible freedom, no longer subject to expectations of conformity. The truth is that it could have been let go of long ago. Gloria Steinem, feminist and aging proponent said this: "Women may be the one group that grows more radical with age." Letting go will do that to you.

Lao Tzu, Eastern philosopher, had this to say about the benefits of letting go: "In the end, the treasure of life is missed by those who hold on and gained by those who let go." Don't you want to find the treasure in life? And now more than ever, if you haven't up until now? Then you'll have to start letting go of attachments.

Something big to let go of is regrets. Regrets are wishing the past to be different than it is. You can wish and wish and wish but the past won't change. What you can change is your reaction to things that happened in the past. As you can choose your reactions to present events and circumstances, so can you change them for ones that happened long ago. With a longer perspective, you can begin to see things in a positive light, seeing the lessons they imparted. The scar on my face from being bitten in Africa is now a badge of courage. At the time it scared me and my family. Now I have a great story to tell of me as a survivor, not a victim to be pitied. I no longer have to spend any time or energy ruing that day, trying to find what else I or someone else could have done differently to prevent it from happening.

People often have a hard time letting go of the opinion of others. They can be paralyzed when they consider some action, worried about what others will think of them. This may be something you want to do or something you want to obtain. What will the neighbor think if...? First of all, sorry to disappoint you but most people are preoccupied with themselves too much to even notice what you are doing. Second, it's your life to be lived as you see fit. You are the best one to judge if something is appropriate for you or not, if that's even the question. A spiritual teacher of mine, Kennedy Schultz, put it this way: "Your opinion of me is no business of mine."

Practicing forgiveness can be a big part of letting something go. Many people think that by forgiving someone you are letting them off the hook for some personal offense. What you are really doing is letting yourself off the hook, letting yourself move on and not holding on to the negative energy around the event. Edwene

Gaines, a gifted minister in Alabama, is a big believer in the power of doing your forgiveness work in writing, preaching the biblical approach of seventy times seven. She suggests that you write your forgiveness of a person thirty-five times in the morning and thirty-five times in the evening, for at least seven days. If at the end of the week the event still holds a charge for you, do it for another week. She continues this practice as long as it takes to get to forgiveness. For me, instead of needing to exact revenge for whatever occurred, I rely on karma. I believe that the universe will ultimately repay the person for their deed or words, in a much more precise way than I ever could. I do look for the lesson for me in my forgiveness, too, seeking to turn the whole thing into a good thing, instead of dwelling on the bad.

A practice that I have found that helps me let go of something that's stuck in my mind, particularly with an emotion, is to name the feeling. When it is just rattling around in my brain a feeling can become all-encompassing, taking over my thoughts. It helps to put words to the amorphous sensations. It doesn't take much time to come up with a name, I'm not even sure how precise you need to be. Just to say to myself "I'm feeling anxious" puts my mind at ease almost instantaneously. It puts an end to the ceaseless running of my thoughts.

Society puts forth a lot of expectations, and these can be very constraining. Women are expected to be cover-girl beauties all the time, twenty-four hours a day, and to "want it all," children, careers, happy marriages, a house in the Hamptons, etc. Men are expected to provide it all and not express their emotions in doing so. Women clean and cook, while men change the oil in the car and cut the grass, etc., etc. Many of these expectations are of our adult roles, either as children growing up to be adults or as adults themselves. As an elder the roles are less defined. It's time to let go of these expectations, to free yourself of them. Ayn Rand, not my favorite novelist but still on target here, said this: "It's not a question of who is going to let me; it's who is going to stop me." The ultimate gatekeeper is you, not anyone else. Not your mother or father, you. Give yourself permission to let go of societal expectations that chafe on your spirit. You will be surprised at how easy it can be.

I remember the night I was standing in my closet trying to decide on what to wear one night. My favorite pants at the time were jeans with a tiny chalk stripe on them. The shirt I wanted to wear was patterned, but you're never supposed to wear patterns with stripes. I decided that to me they looked good together, and I felt good with them on. I wore them out, despite its meaning I was breaking a fashion rule. That night I became confident in my own sense of style, and my self-confidence grew. Try it for yourself, not necessarily wearing stripes and patterns, but stepping out and making your own rules.

One of the most inspirational quotes I know of regarding taking action is from Wayne Gretzky, hockey great: "You miss 100% of the shots you don't take." Try letting go of an attachment. Give something you love away to someone else who may like it too. Start with a small thing and get used to flexing that muscle. Let go of a small hurt. With practice you will get better at it and it will come easier. Then you can let go of bigger and bigger events from your life, but it takes actively letting them go, doing the work

Life Inventory

Have you ever thought of writing your memoirs? You don't have to do it intending it for anyone else's eyes but your own. Do you think a lot about events in your life and how they shaped you? Have you reviewed those events from where you are today, versus how you felt when they happened?

I have attempted to write my memoirs a couple of times. Two years ago, I really got into it. I felt like all these juicy stories were taking up a lot of my thinking and I needed to get them out of my brain, while they were fresh. I started typing them into the computer and before long I was writing 3,000 words a day. This went on for over a month. I ended up with nearly 100,000 words!

Afterwards I found out that writing like that is a part of becoming an elder. The more formal term is taking a life inventory. What's important is to write from where you are now in life, with the benefit of hindsight, writing about the events and their impact on who you are today. What I found was that my stories had evolved from how I used to think about them. No longer was I the victim in every story, they weren't tales of woe. I could see how they shaped me and now I was able to appreciate the person I am today as the sum of my experiences. They were part of what made me who I am today. I was able to harvest the wisdom contained in the story of my life.

There is a popular poster that says "I am strong, because I've been weak. I am fearless, because I've been afraid. I am wise, because I've been foolish. Wisdom comes from learning from our mistakes." What you are able to do in writing this way is to harvest wisdom from your life, wisdom that you have earned and is personal.

A seminal event in my life was the disease in my legs, Perthes hip, at three and a half years old. I instantly went from a boy who ran everywhere to one who had to learn to scoot across the floor on his stomach. My world changed drastically. The first sign of Perthes hip is intense pain. The dying and roughened end of the leg bone grates in the hip joint instead of rotating smoothly. When I used to look back on its effects I would dwell on how I did not have a typical childhood and how that has affected that rest of my life. When I wrote my latest memoirs, the story came out differently. Yes, it was traumatic, life changing. But now I saw that my strength and perseverance, and even my imagination came from that experience. It made me who I am today.

Carl Jung said this: "I am not what happened to me, I am who I choose to become." You have a choice in how you look at the things that have happened in your life. If you take the opportunity to take a life inventory by writing your memoirs in some form, and you write from the perspective of where and who you are now, you are likely to choose different interpretations than you may have in the past, maybe ones that you have held onto for a long, long time. You cannot change the past, but you can choose to change your view of past events, to possibly find the good in them.

I always like it when a deepening relationship gets to the point of sharing stories of the physical scars on our bodies. It may be because I've got some great scars and stories to tell...

My first memory, of the day I couldn't get out of the car to go to my beloved nursery school, is etched on my brain with pain. The doctor devised a metal A-frame brace to keep my hip joints immobilized, to lessen the pain, until a full diagnosis could be made. Soon after I got home, with my brace on, neighbors, fellow ex-pats down the street from where we lived, offered to show me their new puppies, knowing how much I liked dogs. Uncle Patrick, the dogs' master, held me in his arms as he brought me to the puppies. The mother dog, unsure what my aluminum brace was, bit me in the face, taking out my right cheek. The dogs were Rhodesian ridgebacks, bred for lion hunting. We were living West Africa, so the lion hunting was real, not conceptual. I had been bitten in the face by a lion hunting dog. We drove around for two hours looking for a doctor to sew me up. At the Firestone rubber plantation, the doctor we found was a German ex-pat. After he stitched up my face he told me mother that I'll make a fine German when I grow up, "with a limp and a scar." That didn't help her upset.

I tell that story not just for its drama. I've had to overcome it at least twice. After getting bitten my parents got me a dog, to reduce my fear of dogs. That worked well, for a long time. In a workshop 15 years ago, we were asked to imagine the scariest situation we could think of.

I immediately thought of being bitten again. My imagination worked so well that it reignited my fear of dogs. For about six months afterwards when I was around dogs they would growl at me, sensing my fear. More recently, one of the very first time I was taking our new puppy for a walk, I came upon someone playing with their three grown ridgebacks playing off-leash. I couldn't have them, or my puppy, sense any fear because of the possible reaction to it. I summoned every bit of resolve in my body to escort my dog through the pack, without incident. Whew! Today I see my entire experience with Perthes hip as giving me great strength and perseverance, big assets in my life today.

Louise Hay puts it this way: "Honor the entirety of your journey. Don't wish any of it away. Use it for the betterment of the world." Everything that has happened along the way, everything, has made you who you are today. Everything has a lesson in it. The best way to use all of what you have inside, a unique combination of gifts and experiences, is to become an elder.

How can something traumatic in your life now become a positive aspect of your life? You cannot make something un-happen. But you can change how you frame it, from the perspective you have now of your life, likely a different point of view than you had at the time. The most important part is to look at your life now. How has what was traumatic at the time shaped you into who you are today? Has it made you stronger, wiser, smarter, more empathetic, more heart-based, etc.? Are you able, and willing, to change your interpretation, to one that is inspirational instead of a dis-empowering one? If not, what's holding you back? Let it go.

Being Selfish Is OK

Being selfish has gotten a bad rap. You may have been taught as a young child that it was a bad thing. This usually came with lessons about sharing what we have with others. I thought my father was teaching me to not be selfish, to not put my own needs ahead of someone else's. Years later I realized what he was really requiring was that I put his needs ahead of my own. In addition to learning that being selfish was bad, I learned to dismiss my own needs and wants. It took me a long time to be able to get in touch with my need and want feelings.

At a lecture Ernest Chu, the author of *Soul Currency*, opined that what is really selfish is to not take care of yourself. That's because if you don't take care of yourself you are requiring someone else to take care of you and your needs. Self-care isn't selfish then. If you believe that we are all connected, that we are all one, taking care of yourself is also taking care of the whole. This wisdom has freed me up considerably about taking care of myself and not thinking it's selfish to do so.

Another bit of wisdom, this one from Ram Dass, freed me up even further about labeling selfish actions and thoughts as bad: "Every decision is selfish." I have yet to meet someone, no matter how self-effacing, who never took themselves and their needs into consideration when making a decision. Instead, what's involved is a complex calculation of how much of what I want can I fit in to a decision balanced by also respecting what another wants. How much can I get away with having go my way? If every decision is ultimately selfish in the end, that knowledge gives me greater permission to take into account what I want sooner in my deliberation process.

The better we are at striking a fair balance between what we want and what another party wants, the more often we will get at least some of what we want. If we go for too much, too often, we'll lose future opportunities to attempt to get what we want.

During the last vigorous hurricane season there was a story on NPR about stores choosing to price-gouge patrons for bottled water. Not many stores, but at least some of them, chose to jack up how much they were charging, up to ten times the normal price. The economist said that in the long-term that was a money-losing strategy. After the crisis people would remember which stores had raised prices and which had not. Those that had would lose customers over time to those which had not. Typically, by the next crisis the stores which had price-gouged would be out of business, ultimately helping those stores still in business due to less competition. The stores which were too selfish, not honoring the balance of their needs and those of their customers, may have made more in the short-run of the crisis, but that decision wasn't good in the long-term. Wall Street puts it another, more graphic way: "Hogs get fat, but pigs get slaughtered."

If you accept that every decision is selfish, does that free you up to feel better about being selfish in your affairs? Does it help to realize that other people are also operating the same way, being as selfish as they feel they can safely be?

The poet Khalil Gibran wrote this: "And God said, 'love thy enemy,' and I obeyed and loved myself." How many times have you heard that you are your own worst enemy? Has that helped you to improve? Maybe you should try loving yourself and being a bit selfish and see if that doesn't improve your mood.

Self-care is an important aspect of being an elder. Even if we have spent our entire adult life with a mate, it is likely that you will end up alone at the end of your life. Then you will have neither someone to care for you not someone to care for. Your care will be up to you. Why not learn now what taking care of yourself involves?

Anna Madrigal, Armistead Maupin's character in his Tales of the City series, said this: "All life is maintenance." Many of us take better care of our cars than we do ourselves. I have found in life that that which you do not take care of initially, if it doesn't go away on its own, gets worse until it's addressed. Part of maturing is knowing what will just go away and what will not, and to be aware of your own level of denial about body sensations.

At a class last week, the instructor, a gifted spiritual practitioner, offered me a private one-on-one session to discuss manifesting abundance, the class' subject. Afraid to be selfish, my knee-jerk reaction was "no, thanks." I thought about what a chicken I that night after class was and the next morning. Like often happens, the instructor had also been thinking of me, but on a different topic. I responded to her email with a call. It turned into the one-on-one session I so desired but was afraid to admit. It was an amazing call, with several big "aha" moments for me. Being selfish was good for me, and she got out of the call what she wanted, too.

You hereby have my permission to become more selfish, more self-caring, from here on out! (You're already doing it anyway...)

Power of Belief

When I first met with the minister of my new spiritual home he had me speak a lot about my interpretation of the world. His conclusion was that I lacked faith. As a result, for a long time I looked for ways of growing my faith, finding little to guide me. When we got a new minister, one of his first talks was about how we all have faith, in something. It may be faith that the world works in our favor, or that it does not work that way. We may have faith in ourselves, or in others, not ourselves. We may have faith in God, faith in Mother Nature, or faith in science. The real question is what do you have faith in?

This is another opportunity to tease out of your subconscious what your assumptions are. As you make a decision, a small or a big one, examine your internal logic. When you are finding a parking space, what do you have faith in? Are you confident you'll find one easily, or are they hard to find? Whichever way you think, it will influence your interpretation of events. If you think it's going to be easy, the space you find will be an easy one to find. If you think it's going to be hard, it will be hard, even if it's the same parking space.

On a visit to my parents a friend of theirs told me this story. He was friends with the man who was the Macy's Thanksgiving Day Parade's Santa Claus for several decades. "Santa" lived in Pennsylvania and his entire family would go each year to New York for the parade. One year

"Santa's" eldest son had just turned sixteen. He went to his mother and asked if he could help dad this year? She replied that they would all be going to the parade to help, like they had each past year. The son replied "No, can I help dad deliver the presents?" The son believed his father really was Santa Claus, despite lots of evidence to the contrary. That is the power of belief. It colors what we see and experience in the world, whether or not your belief is true, because it's true for you!

The first quest then is to find out what beliefs you hold. Then, when they come to be conscious, you can check them to see if they still work for you today, or not. If not, then it's your choice what you believe, what you have faith in.

But what if it's not true? You've already seen with Santa that you can believe sincerely in something that's not true. You, yourself, may have believed in Santa Claus once. Or the Easter Bunny, or the Tooth Fairy, or in monsters. An example is the belief that humans couldn't run a sub-four-minute mile. Once that record fell, with Roger Banister breaking it in 1954, soon after several other runners did it, too. Today the record is down to 3:43:13.

Beliefs are not truths. They are what we choose to believe, true or not, conscious or not. What is "true" can change over time. Galileo was found "vehemently suspect of heresy" and spent the last years of his life living under house arrest for his support of the idea that the Earth revolves around the Sun. So much for the truth. What beliefs do you hold today that will be proven untrue tomorrow?

In Harv Eker's book *The Secrets of the Millionaire Mind* he writes about the limiting beliefs we humans have. He posits that if acorns had the mind of humans you would rarely see and oak tree over ten feet tall. Having limiting beliefs, such as "I'm not worthy," keeps you from reaching your full human potential. Such beliefs must be brought into consciousness and then examined thoroughly. Are they "true" for us today? Are they beneficial to our lives? If not, let them go. Replace them with beliefs that are empowering, so you begin to grow to your full potential.

In my early thirties I noticed that if I was at a social event at night, I would begin to get crabby, wanting to go home no matter how much fun I was having, at about 9:30 p.m. It was causing some strife with my mate, a natural night person versus my natural morning person. As I reviewed my thoughts, I recalled my mother's admonitions about not being a "dirty stay-out." What that was, was never fleshed out for me, but I knew it was "bad." Along with that she would say that "the only hours of sleep that count are the ones before midnight." So, I deduced that a dirty stay-out was one who didn't get any sleep that counted, staying out past midnight. In the back of my mind, unconsciously, I was afraid of what would happen to me if I didn't get to sleep before midnight. This was contrary to my own experience, that on occasion I was OK staying up late. All of a sudden, I began to question all the statements my mother had made. Were they really true, or not? I suggest this is a good place to start – what wisdom did your parents repeat to you that you now take as gospel truth? Some of those beliefs may be limiting ones, stunting your growth, your evolution.

One of my beliefs is that I'm not very coordinated. This comes from half my life by the time I was seven-years-old being spent with casts, braces and crutches. In the 1990s, when so many people were dying of AIDS, a friend who was HIV-positive, carrying the HIV virus, was afraid that he, too, was soon to die. One item on his bucket list was to hang-glide. He had found a half-price offer from a nearby facility that taught hang-gliding and he convinced a group of us to go along with him.

The first weekend of lessons started on flat ground, running with the kite on our shoulders, giving us the sensation of the kite actually flying. Once we had that down we got on a bunny hill, attempting to launch from about ten feet in elevation above the field in front of us. It was clear to everyone that I was the worst pilot, unable to make a flight without crashing quickly, often veering way off to one side or another. I took it as further evidence of my lack of coordination.

Having had the slightest feeling of what it was like to fly, something I had been fantasizing about my entire life, I really wanted to learn how to fly a hang-glider. Over several years we took different groups up to Lookout Mountain a couple of times a year to try hang-gliding. Some people from the initial group kept going, others would try it once and be done with it.

Much to my surprise, I was the first to be told that I had successfully completed the training and now I was OK to launch solo off the cliff. I had been to the launch site many times. It was a twenty-foot square of concrete straddling the edge of the mountain. On one end it was sitting on the flat ground. At the other end was a two-hundred-foot drop. Eighteen-hundred feet below was the landing area, a grass field. In the many times I'd been on the launch pad I had never gotten myself to the edge of it, afraid of falling off it. Just the thought of it makes my heart swell with anticipation. Now I was about to run off the end of it, with a big kite strapped to my back.

At Lookout Mountain they train more people than anywhere else in the world to solo hang-glide. I was having a hard time believing that I was really ready to solo. Didn't they know how uncoordinated I was? What finally switched my mind was the knowledge that the instructor believed I could do it, and that he had trained many pilots before me.

I summoned all the courage I could find and set up my hang-glider. I checked every fastener four different times, just to be sure. I didn't want to take off and find that my glider was flying but that I wasn't attached to it and would plummet to my death once my arms tired of hanging on. As I had learned, I ran off the end of the launch pad with the wing already lifting off my shoulders. The kite began to dive, and I pulled the control bar in, speeding my descent, counter-intuitively. Soon enough I leveled-out and was flying, soaring over the valley. It was glorious, the sensation of flight. And really not scary.

All evening I kept looking up to where I had launched from, from down in the valley where were staying. I was still trying to fathom that I, the totally uncoordinated scaredy-cat, had actually ran off the concrete pad I had never before gotten myself to even the edge of. It was the week of my birthday. Instead of feeling old, the oldest of my friends there, I was feeling empowered. This old dog had learned a new trick. And I wasn't as uncoordinated as I had believed myself to be. I had risked mortal danger, despite what I thought might happen to me, and lived to tell about it.

My therapist at the time loved the story. Whenever I would get stuck subsequently, she would remind me that I had already risked life and limb. My current challenging belief was likely not as scary as running off the side of a mountain had been. Darn, she was right!

A poster I saw recently expanded on the power of belief this way: "Your mind will believe everything you tell it. Feed it faith. Feed it truth. Feed it with love." You choose your beliefs, whether you believe that or not. The more you can bring what you believe, what you have faith in, into consciousness, the more you have the power to upgrade to what you believe to be true for you now, from the perspective of years and context.

Acceptance

Another way to look at "It's all good" is as acceptance of what is. The difference between the two is that in "It's all good" you have some expectation that at some point you will see the good that comes out of everything, including circumstances that at the time don't look very good. Whereas with accepting what is, you just accept the circumstances without necessarily expecting good to come of them. There is a total lack of judgement, things just are what they are. Accepting what is takes "It's all good" to another level, one of further detachment.

It is said that what you resist persists. Buddhists phrase it "If you focus on the hurt, you will continue to suffer. If you focus on the lesson, you will continue to grow." If you mull over and over again in your mind something that happened to you, you don't let it go and it stays around, in your consciousness. You have experienced how fleeting feelings of joy and happiness are. They seem to come and just as quickly go. They do not persist. That's because you are welcoming them, not resisting them. Like any emotion that you don't choose to dwell on, they pass on by as quickly as they came to you.

Accepting what is does not mean indifference or apathy. It doesn't mean not looking at what has happened or been said. But this examination is not looking to fault someone, yourself or another. The focus is on the lesson. How does something inform you further about yourself and the way the world operates?

I used to look at my years with Perthes hip and its treatments as devastating to my formation as a full human being, permanently scaring me. Through writing my memoirs recently and the space of time, I now see it as still quite formative, making me who I am today, but in a positive light. It made me stronger and more sensitive to my surroundings. These traits are of value to me today and have been my entire life, even when I did not necessarily view them that way.

You may wish parts of your life to have a different ending than they did, up until now. When you are able to review them from where you stand today, who you are today, you will likely see them as advantageous, not detrimental. They contained the seeds of important aspects of you, assets today. It is said "sometimes you win, and sometimes you grow." You can and should learn from your wins in addition to your "losses," but life offers more lessons when you fall short of your goal. How can you better prepare for the next time something similar happens? The abundant repetition of nature ensures that there will be a next time, and a next, until you find the lesson and evolve your consciousness.

When you react to something, including a memory, with negative thoughts instead of positive ones, you encode the event with more negativity than was perhaps there originally, making it worse. This can grow like a snowball you roll in the snow, bigger and bigger. When you are feeling down your mind will hunt for similar feelings to reinforce where you are. You can be flooded with "bad" memories. Such ruminations make the situation worse, not better. When I get depressed it feels like I cannot find a solid step on which to find my footing. What builds up is the negativity, where I cannot see anything good. If instead you find the lesson in something, you are informed by memories, not overwhelmed with their negative attachments. Then when you are reminded of something it is likely because of its similarity, seeing a pattern, and the lesson learned before may apply to the situation you find yourself in currently.

A place where I have learned to accept things as they are is playing backgammon on the computer. I am a pretty aggressive player, which means from time to time I lose spectacularly. I may be going along fine until the computer gets a couple of perfect dice rolls. The dice seem to favor the computer player, but I just have to accept them as they come up. I still get riled up from time to time, but it's been a great way to practice this skill and strengthen that muscle for when it really matters.

Does acceptance of what is absolve you of responsibility? No, it does not. Should you feel guilty about what you did? Guilt is the dark side of responsibility, where you can beat yourself up about something you did, and that's not a constructive response. Whereas taking responsibility means things are still in play and there is something you can do about them.

A story I've heard that distinguishes between responsibility and guilt is one of a monk who lived on the outskirts of his village. One day he opened his front door and found a baby in a basket there. He had no guilt about the baby being there, but he was now responsible for its well-being. He had a choice to make about what to do with the baby. He decided to take the baby in and to care for it. The story continues, with someone knocking at his door a year later. The person there now wanted the baby back. In an extreme example of letting go he relinquished the baby and went about his life.

The monk's tale is also one of detaching from forces outside his control. He took responsibility without questioning where the baby had come from, something outside of him. Nor did he fight to keep the baby when he was asked to give it up a year later, again something not in his control.

Another layer of accepting what is as it is, is being comfortable with yourself, as you are. Barbra Streisand puts it this way: "*It gets easier as you get older. You accept yourself for who you are – your flaws and attributes. It's easier to live in your own skin.*" This requires a lot of letting go, especially as your body changes as you age. Ram Dass wonders why we can see the beauty in a wizened tree, shaped by its environment and still alive, but not in the wrinkles in an old face, also shaped by its environment and still very much alive. As your skin get wrinkles, as your knees ache with arthritis, as your back hurts from years of work, can you still see the beautiful soul you are. Stanislaw Jerzy Lec, a Polish poet, put it wonderfully: "*Youth is a gift of nature, but old age is a work of art.*"

One of the biggest parts of life to accept is your mortality. This is a critical element in the path to becoming an elder. For me, my denial was wiped away witnessing my friends die of AIDS. I could no longer believe that I was immortal, immune to death. It was going to come anyway, no matter how "good" I might try to be. What you don't know is when your time is coming. That's part of the mystery of death. It's part of what we have to accept.

Counter-intuitively, accepting your own mortality frees you up to live a fuller life. Really knowing that any day could be your last, how would you spend your time, what would you say to whom? Did you spend today that way? If not, why not? Today could be your last day.

A friend of mine spent his senior year of high school as an exchange student in Bolivia, in a small town. Every weekday his family would work, take a siesta, eat together, dance together, and spend time talking to each other. What I got was that these people knew how to live like today's your last day. The sad story of American men dying within months of their retirement is too common. They likely put off enjoying life while they worked so hard, only to have their leisure years snatched away from them by death. And now it seems that women's lifespans are beginning to mimic men's, with more heart disease. Do you know that when we were hunter gatherers we only worked about twenty hours per week?

What does being afraid of dying gain you? Nothing but a bunch of worry over another thing that you have no control over. No one has ever skipped death, no one has survived life. We are living longer these days, but not forever. Julius Caesar has this to say: "*Cowards die many times before their actual death.*" Cowards haven't yet learned to accept their mortality and fear has them miss out on the fullness of life.

When I took my mate to my alma mater, Yale, for the first time, he was in awe. He kept commenting on the grandeur of the place as we walked the campus. We ventured into the main library and he couldn't believe the scale and beauty of the main desk, which looks a lot like a gilded altar, thirty feet tall. Then he asked about a smallish building. It was the rare book library, and I'd never been in it myself. Its walls are stone and look solid white from the outside. When we walked in my mate was certain that this was center of all learning, the seat of all wisdom. From the inside the solid exterior glows with subdued colors as sunlight penetrates the marble panels. In the display cases where he expected to find the deepest wisdom, my mate found illustrated volumes of Peter Pan, a long-time personal favorite of his. The biggest volume was open to the quote from Peter Pan himself: "To die would be an awfully big adventure!" Can you look at the unknowns of death with anticipation like that?

An important step in making peace with death is writing a will and making final arrangements. Some people have detailed plans of how they want their funeral to be, including the music to be played in each part of the service. If you think that you have fully accepted what is, but haven't written down such details, leaving it to others, you're not all the way there yet.

Making peace with dying doesn't mean you have to stop living, not at all. Native Americans say that if you're still here you still have more to do. Maya Angelou wrote that "As long as you're breathing, it's never too late to do some good."

Wisdom

Wisdom is one of those things that is hard to define, but easy to recognize when you hear it. A definition, from the Berlin Wisdom Project, is "an expert knowledge system concerning the fundamental pragmatics of life." Another more general one is "maintaining positive well-being and kindness in the face of challenges." If there ever was a stage of life when wisdom is useful it is as an elder, a time when physical and/or mental challenges can be a present. It has been said that the wisdom of old age can more than make up for the erosion of other attributes.

Scientifically, wisdom comes as better recognition of patterns of behavior and from more nuanced responses, based on an accumulation of experiences. David Mamet puts it this way: "Old age and treachery will always beat youth and exuberance." While treachery isn't my favorite synonym for wisdom, knowing more about how the world operates might feel that way to someone on the receiving end of a wise move.

How do you cultivate the wisdom of your years? The best way is to review your life, to recognize patterns and trends. The best way to do that is to write some memoirs. As I've said before, you don't have to write for anyone else's eyes. You may not even read them again once you've written your life down. Or you may feel that what you've written could be important to the world and needs to be disseminated further. You are a unique individual who has insights no one else has the same perspective on, and what you've written may contain wisdom that it timely and important. When you start you may only want to write about a specific incident, not your entire life. That's fine, too. A lot of people think that hand-writing is best, that it taps into your core better. I prefer using my computer, so I can move parts around and do some editing as I write.

As I've already written, when I started such a project for the third time, so far at least, it was like I was possessed, typing furiously, 3,000 words a day. Events that I wanted to be sure to include kept popping into my head and I quickly jotted them down, so I wouldn't lose them as fast as they came to mind. I could think of little else.

The primary insight I got was that I had reinvented myself many times, taking on new courses in life. It usually involved wanting to emphasize some aspect of myself or wanting to discard a piece that had proven to be maladaptive. Often it involved a physical move or a new endeavor. Sometimes it was more conscious than others.

When I moved to Ft. Lauderdale at the end of 1985 I came to start a new job. It felt good to know an employer wanted me and my experiences. I got there knowing one person, someone I'd met when I had visited Ft. Lauderdale for my interview. Starting with him I met his friends and picked out a favorite whom I found interesting. I got to know them a bit and met their friends, again choosing one or two to get to know better. I felt like I was consuming people, and I felt a little callous doing it. In the process I met two of the most influential people in my life, a mentor and my mate. I also made lifelong friends with a several other people. I recast myself and my life, as I had done before and have done since, more than once, emphasizing or de-emphasizing some aspect of my life up until then.

The philosopher Jean-Jacques Rousseau of the 18th century had this to say: "What wisdom can you find that is greater than kindness?" Such kindness, towards both those we know and those we don't, comes from learning that each person has things in their life that are less than perfect, and yet they continue to be part of the world. You cannot know when someone is having a bad day, when it is taking some processing time to get back to the attitude that

"It's all good." And everyone may not realize when you aren't at your best. I remember being at college, having a really bad day and feeling like I had to be radiating my foul mood, when someone would out of the blue complement me on my smile. Didn't they see how awful I felt? How could I be smiling with all that was on my mind? Perhaps the comment was a reminder from the universe that things weren't quite as dour as I was imagining them to be. Kindness, gentleness, was just what I needed at the time.

Another piece of wisdom that I recognized in writing my memoirs was that as intelligent as I may be, when I made a decision based solely on the facts and not on feelings, it was often a bad one. Marc Chagall, the artist, put it this way: "When I create from the heart, nearly everything works; if from the head, nearly nothing."

My bout with Perthes hip had me attempt to cut off feelings from my body as much as possible, in an attempt to avoid further pain. My seventh session of Rolfing, massaging my muscles back to their original alignment and shape, began with my neck and head. Within the first few minutes of the ninety-minute session waves began in my body from my neck down to my toes as my body reintegrated itself. The Rolfer and I could see and feel the waves. I have since learned to better feel and trust the signals my body picks up. I'm not saying that Rolfing is required for you to find your wisdom, but it was a definite part of my path to wholeness, reconnecting to my heart, my feelings.

The best quote I've found about wisdom is from a 17th century Spanish philosopher, Baltasar Gracian. He said that "A wise man does at once what a fool does finally." This economy of effort suits elders well. They have less energy and less time for lollygagging. When I have a dilemma in my life that I need to figure out my first action is the one I know that will solve the crisis, instead of the easiest possible solution that may work.

The wisdom you find from your life isn't just a benefit to you. One of an elder's roles is to bring such wisdom to their community. This may be in the form of their longer-term perspective, having seen life evolve over many years, recognizing its ebb and flow. It may be from certain stories from the "old days" that are suddenly relevant today. A personal goal I set at about age thirty-five was to be regarded as a wise man by my peers. I now understand that wisdom continues to come to those who cultivate it, something I am still doing, and expect to do until I leave this plane of existence.

Spirituality

Spirituality is defined as "the quality of being concerned with the human spirit or soul as opposed to material or physical things." To me, this is the sweet spot in becoming an elder, being able to concentrate on spirituality instead of pursuing more doing and more possessions. As a friend of mine says, you can only have so many couches.

Many people wish to explore their spirituality, their relationship to the world outside themselves, but don't have the time. When you are working hard building a career and raising a family it can be difficult to set aside space in your day for quiet contemplation. As people get older some of their obligations begin to shrink.

Maybe you have the opportunity to retire, ceasing to work at all. At some point your family grows up to the point of self-sufficiency, perhaps leaving you an empty nester. While both of these are huge adjustments to your life, they do serve to free up parts of your day for other things.

An aspect of being an elder is a focus on spirituality of some sort. But it's not just time contemplating your navel, it's also living a life that demonstrates to others what a spiritual life looks like, "walking the talk." Such living is good for the elder and good for your community. This is one of the differences between being elderly and being an elder. This focus allows elders to flourish despite living in an aging body with an aging mind.

Having a spiritual practice is a good place to start to explore your spirituality. Such a practice is an everyday event, a regular time of the day to get re-centered and reconnected to oneself. It could be walk or some time in a comfortable chair away from everyone else. What you do in that time isn't nearly as important as the regularity of it. Of course, it's alright to miss a day on occasion, but after a while you really won't want to. Johann Wolfgang von Goethe, a prominent German writer, said this: "This is the highest wisdom that I own; freedom and life are earned by those alone who conquer them each day anew." Spirituality is not a one-time thing, something you attain and have from then on. It is something you must keep alive, keep growing. To be an elder is to explore and demonstrate spirituality as a core part of your life every day.

Meditation may be part of your spiritual practice. Meditation can take many forms and the breadth of ways to do it can be explore until you find one that works for you. A good way to start is with guided meditation, where someone is quietly talking you through the time you are sitting still. There are numerous applications available on your smart-phone that can provide guided meditations, or you can get a CD. There are forms of meditation that you do with your eyes open, and many that you do with your eyes closed. The idea is to quiet your mind. Having a quiet mind doesn't necessarily mean one that has no thoughts. It's more like still having thoughts but not grabbing onto them to examine them. A thought floats into your consciousness and you let it float out, without dwelling on the thought. As you practice this gets easier. It is amazing to me how quickly even a very charged thought can disappear, if you don't start to mull it over.

Something akin to meditation is yoga. Yoga seems like it is primarily a physical thing. It can be a great way to move your body and help keep you limber. The exercise part gives your mind something to do, to get lost in. But the real aim is to quiet your mind. Like with meditation there are many forms of yoga, many to be explored until you find one that suits you and your life.

I find yoga and meditation to be like mini-vacations. Whatever is bothering you at the start is forgotten in the process, giving you a break. Such breaks bring relief from churning thoughts and often allows space for a previously unavailable idea or solution to come into consciousness. I have experienced many times being stuck in a dark corner, thinking there's no way out, and meditating or doing yoga and having a new idea rescue me from the deep recesses of my repetitive thoughts.

A big part of spirituality is gratitude, being thankful for what you have, a form of accepting what is. The spiritual principle is that why would the universe grant you with more if you're not happy with what it has already provided. Oprah Winfrey puts it this way: "Be thankful for what you have; you'll end up having more. If you concentrate on what you don't have, you will never, ever have enough." It has been said that the simplest prayer is just "Thank you!" Spending your day repeating "thank you" in your mind is a great way to get into the habit of gratitude.

The opposite of gratitude is complaining. Complaining keeps alive something that happened in the past. It's also adding more negative emotion to it, instead of letting it pass. It's one thing to review something and come up with something you can do yourself to improve the situation. Often, that improvement is with yourself, not the one you're complaining about. You have control of yourself but not of what the other person does.

Watching the words you use is another aspect of spirituality. As you have probably already learned, you cannot take back words said. Instead, here I mean the specific words you use, like "never" and "hate." They are strong words which leave little room for others to live in. If you say you are never going to do something, you don't allow for yourself or others to evolve.

Saying you hate something adds a lot of negativity, so much so that it may ricochet on you. Sigmund Freud said that a phobia is as strong as a wish. Having something in mind to maintain a hate of it may call up the very thing you don't want.

Patience is another spiritual practice. Patience, like gratitude, is another form of accepting what is. I used to be very impatient. I came to realize that when I hurried things up, instead of letting them take their natural course, I would get a result, but rarely the one I wanted. If I would do my part and then let events unfold on their own, I usually got a lot closer to my desired outcome, if not something better. If there was more work on my part required I would do it, but I wouldn't micromanage each step of the way. Previously I had thought my constant scrutiny was a necessary and good part. Eventually I realized it was counterproductive. I was advising a client who enjoyed entering sweepstakes. She felt like she could do more to increase her odds of winning. We finally agreed that her part included a positive attitude while filling out and mailing her entries was as much as she could do, nothing more. After that she had to let events progress naturally. Now, when I'm with my family they are astounded by my patience, compared to how I used to be.

Closely related to patience is an attitude of doing my part immediately when something comes up, instead of waiting for a more opportune time. Spiritually, if I don't do my part when first presented, I'm delaying the natural unfolding. My lack of immediate action has consequences, too, usually unfavorable ones. Often if I delay acting I forget to do my part later. When I don't feel like doing my part now, I rarely feel more like doing it later. I have found that the best way to feel like starting something is to start doing it. Otherwise I can agonize over not doing something for much longer than it actually takes to do the thing in the first place. A practice of mine when I have a list of things I need to get done is to first identify how long the period of time I have to work on my list. Then I allocate time to each item, giving each item some time, even if it's not as much as I think the item may take. I assign an order to the tasks, sometimes in order of priority. More often it will be in an order that moves from an easy item to a harder one, giving the hardest ones an earlier slot to get them out of the way. Then I commit to working my list, but only so long on each item as I have identified. It constantly amazes me how quickly many of the items get done in much less time than allocated. All I really needed to do was to get started on them and they were thus much easier than I had imagined. Amelia Earhart put it this way: "The most difficult thing is the decision to act, the rest is merely tenacity."

Ram Dass is one of my favorite teachers. He is very real in that he readily admits that he has done some crazy things in his life, like mushrooms. Having had a debilitating stroke twenty years ago, he continues to lecture and write, demonstrating that one can be a wise elder despite limitations. He had this to say about his spiritual life: "I would like my life to be a statement of love and compassion – and where it is not, that's where my work lies."

There is always more spiritual work to be done, more growth to be had.

There's been a lot written recently about the power of being present, living in the now. Some people are consumed by the past, keeping it alive and in the present for themselves, often missing out on the joy of life that is all around them. Some people seem to live in the future, waiting for something outside themselves to happen, like winning the lottery. They are putting off living, again missing much of what is being offered them. A business group I belonged to concluded its first meeting with a raffle, picking a business card out of a jar. The person whose card was drawn had already left. Very quickly it was decided that "you must be present to win." This became the only rule of the group, having much broader implications than just with drawings for door prizes. Being present is a key element of spirituality and being an elder.

On September 11, 2001 I woke up in a lodge in the Grand Canyon National Park. Friends had gathered in Las Vegas the weekend before to celebrate a fortieth birthday in Sin City. Three of us had extended our trip, driving a rental car over the Hoover Dam and on to the Grand Canyon. We ate our breakfast and went to the corral where we were scheduled to take a mule ride down into the canyon. When we came out of the canyon that afternoon we found out what tragedy had struck while we were out of touch. For a long time, I wondered why I was in such a place, probably one of the safest in the country, on that fateful day. Fifteen years later, on a business trip to Colorado, I realize why. It was to emphasize the centrality of being in nature to my life. Being in nature often, is an important component of spirituality and being an elder. When I have a burning question on my mind I like to take a walk outside or to sit by a stream and just be with nature. Nature has already solved most of the dilemmas of life. The answers are just waiting to be found. Getting out doesn't have to mean going to the Grand Canyon. Just getting outside, outside of one's concrete cocoon can be enough.

Activating one's creativity is part of being an elder. For many of us it's been a long time since we did something creative. School seems to teach most of us that we are not creative, not artists. I disagree. Creation is a vital part of yourself and your life. I'm a big proponent of reactivating our creative parts in your elderhood. It doesn't have to be painting masterpiece oil paintings to count. Sewing, drawing, doodling and photography are all easily accessed and they all get the creative juices flowing again. For myself I have chosen two primary creative outlets, tie-dyeing and building mobiles. I started tie-dyeing because I feel men's pants are very boring, that I wanted more color. It has expanded from there. The process is fun because you never know what you're going to get, it's always a surprise. It's also fun to wear clothes that are my own creation. I couldn't have been happier the day my sister, who doesn't always appreciate my colorful clothes, and I went to see an exhibit of Picasso sculptures. In addition to the art on display a number of people noticed the art I was wearing, complementing me on it. Wow! The mobiles are yard art, hung from a tree in our front yard, much to the chagrin of some of our neighbors. Many like the pieces, made out of found objects that were once in junk-piles but are now pretty again.

With creativity goes beauty, learning to see it everywhere. Albert Einstein said: "There are only two ways to live your life: as though nothing is a miracle, or as though everything is a miracle." I prefer the latter. There is beauty all around us and igniting your creativity will help you see it, too. The miracle of life is all around you, whether it's a flower blooming in the spring, or a leafless tree in winter, both teeming with life, one on the outside and one on the inside. The beauty of life is in you, too, even if you no longer fit in some of your clothes. Coco Chanel, the French designer, said: "Beauty begins the moment you decide to be yourself."

If there was ever a time to decide to be yourself, freer of society's expectations than ever before, it's as an elder. It's time for your own personal style, and to wear it with grace and elegance, even if it's your mom jeans. Sofia Loren, the film actress, said this: "Beauty is how you feel inside, and it's reflected in your eyes. It is not something physical."

A wonderful musician, Bob Sima, has a song entitled "Healed people heal people." By living a life filled with spiritual pursuit, walking the talk, we demonstrate to others the richness of life available to those who pursue the path to becoming an elder. By living your life "out loud," whatever that means to you, you are an example to others who aren't quite there yet. You don't have to say a word.

Obstacles

One of the books I'd like to write is one entitled "Learned Instincts." It's an oxymoron of sorts as instincts are generally hard-wired, things you're born with, not learned ones. I do think you can learn things in a way that they become like instincts, natural. Usually a really bad experience, or maybe a really good one, teaches us something that we then incorporate into our being. I have also seen in myself that such deep learning is not easy.

On the path to becoming an elder you will encounter obstacles. You may find it easier to return to the denial of your aging. Confronting the negative stereotypes of aging people may leave you exhausted and overwhelmed, causing you to fall prey to them instead of choosing to forge your own way. The personal work described in this book may take longer than you like. A favorite refrigerator magnet of mine says "God grant me patience, but please hurry!" Unfortunately, patience doesn't come that way.

More generally, it can be hard to change, no matter what the topic. You have a lot of personal inertia propelling you in a certain direction, the one you're already on. The people in your life also have the expectation that tomorrow you will be the same person you were today, serving to constrain you to your current path.

What do you do when the going gets tough? Do you persevere, or do return to the way you've always done things, not staying with a newly discovered bit of wisdom? If you're like me, you'll often stop trying at the first sign of difficulty. How many times do you do things the way your used to doing them, even though you know there's a better way?

The best way I have found to keep me on track, to keep me from falling into old ways of doing something, is to have someone to travel the path with, a guide. An African proverb says: "If you want to go fast, go alone. If you want to travel far, go together." The path to becoming an elder is a life-long one, a far travel. If you want to take that journey it's best to go with someone else. When I am making changes to my life, I find I'm more likely to be successful if I have someone else to be accountable to. It's too easy to quit if I'm the only one keeping up with my progress.

History is littered with smart people who had a hard time in life, being less than successful. Knowing what to do does not always translate into doing what you know to do. In scuba-diving class you learn the adage "Plan your dive and dive your plan." It is not in knowing how to become an elder that the richness of a full life comes. It is by applying this knowledge that you get the benefits. Leonardo da Vinci said it this way: "Knowing is not enough; we must apply. Being willing is not enough; we must do."

Marching Orders

Thank you for reading all the way to this point! What you have seen is that the path to become an elder involves a lot of personal work. You have been challenged to see that "It's all good," all the time. You have seen that you always have choices, that the world in far from just black and white. The task of writing your memoirs has been given you, as a way to harvest the personal wisdom that you have seen in all your years. The value of letting go, of everything, has been described. Being selfish has moved from being a bad thing to be a good and necessary one. The incredible power of belief, and the ready ability to alter your beliefs, one Santa Claus at a time, has been shown. The need to accept what is, including your mortality, has been explained. There is personal wisdom for you to gather from your experiences and you now know how to do find it. The richness of life in the pursuit of spirituality has been dangled in front of you. Now what do you do with that new knowledge?

Have you thrown yourself a Jubilee party? If not, why not? How did it make you feel? What did you learn from the experience, and what your friends had to say about you? If you have, be sure to email me at Book@theSpiritualElders.com to tell me about your party.

The world I envision coming is one where elders have regained their place as valued and vital members of society. Demographics are pushing this vision, with the Baby Boom generation now reaching the age of seventy at the rate of 10,000 per day for the next twenty years. Problems with the modern world, to which we are still adapting to, are calling forth the wisdom and guidance of elders. Instead of a world where elders need to yell angrily to get the attention they deserve the same as everyone else, I see one where when elders speak they are heard and heeded. I see elders given value as elders, not as older adults struggling to stay youthful to be relevant. Multi-generational events are commonplace, easy to find.

Now it's up to you to do the work of becoming an elder. A rich last third of your life, one full of purpose and meaning, with an important role in your family and community, awaits you.

To help with the process I've written a Workbook to go with this book. It poses questions that go with each chapter. If you would like to have a copy of the workbook, follow this link:

https://tinyurl.com/I-Hate-Getting-Old-WORKBOOK

Thank you!

Love and hugs!

Karl Gustafson, Elder-in-Training

Book@theSpiritualElders.com

Made in the USA
Columbia, SC
19 January 2019